The Walking Rebel
Micropoems and Poems

Sushant Thapa

Transcendent Zero Press
Houston, Texas

Library of Congress Control Number: 2025936029
ISBN-13: 978-1-946460-63-9

The Walking Rebel
Micropoems and Poems

Sushant Thapa

Other Titles by the Author

Poetry

The Poetic Burden and Other Poems (Authorspress, New Delhi, 2020)

Abstraction and Other Poems (Impspired, UK, 2021)

Minutes of Merit (Haoajan, Kolkata, 2021)

Love's Cradle (World Inkers Printing and Publishing, New York, USA and Senegal, Africa, 2023)

Spontaneity: A New Name of Rhyme (Ambar Publication House, New Delhi, 2023)

Chorus of Simplicity and Other New Poems (Ukiyoto Publishing, 2024)

Finding My Soul in Kathmandu (Ukiyoto Publishing, 2024)

Flash fiction and Short stories

The One Rupee Taker and Other Stories (Ukiyoto Publishing, 2024)

Acknowledgements

I extend my gratitude to following magazines and journals for publishing some of the poems in this book: International Times (UK), Bold Monkey Review (Australia), Sacred Chickens Blog, Medusa's Kitchen (USA), World Inkers Network (New York, USA and Dakar, Senegal, Africa), English Sahitya Post (Nepal), European Poetry, Polis Magazino (Greece), Learning and Creativity (India), Sindh Courier (Pakistan), The Beatnik Cowboy (Denver, Colorado, USA), The Wise Owl Magazine (India) and Masticadores USA.

Awards Received by the Author

Indology Best Poet Award 2022, West Bengal, India

Yashaswi Book Awards 2022, Nepal

Sahitto Award (Winner of the Jury Award 2023), Bangladesh

Kamala-Raj Bahadur Literature Award-2024 (Biratnagar, Nepal)

Contents

Art of Living 15

Friendship................................16

Death 17

Bird in the Sky 18

The Presence of the Damned 19

A Monument of Meaning 20

Freedom................................21

Seclusion 22

Readers 23

Shaking Hands 24

All the Way 25

Without You 26

Banishing Desires 27

Fame 28

Taking Opportunities 29

Efforts Underway 30

My Temptations 31

My Slumber 32

My Pedestal 33

Letting Go 34

The Grass Is Always Green 35

Cloudy Haze 36

Hunger 37

My Carrier 38

Confession 39

To Keep Moving 40

My Love 41

Tiredness 42

Poverty 43

Poetry 44

Love 45

Agony 46

Dream 47

Explanation 48

Smile 49

Perspective 50

The Last Rebel 51

Addiction 52

Writing...53

Sadness 54

Life 55

Habit 56

Discovery...57

Endurance 58

The Age 59

Health 60

Books & My Thoughts.........................61

Ruled by Clowns................................62

Bouquet of Life or Death.....................63

When Words Make Love............................64

Cup of Loneliness.................................65

January Winter...................................66

Expensive Humanity..............................67

The Common Rain 68

Loving Someone...................................69

Time That Followed Me............................70

Crafting Love....................................71

Holding Love Souls...............................72

Looking at the World 73

Such Winter......................................74

A Poem in the Dark 75

Theatre full of Love.............................76

The Family Photo Album..........................77

Beholding Love...................................78

Sorrow Is a River................................79

Art and Discontents..............................80

Favorable Conditions.............................81

Multifaceted Life 82

Claps from Strangers 84

Reason to Love 85

Wind: A Musical Healer 86

Majestic in Absence 87

Let Me Feel Alive 88

Swimming Waters 89

Nectar of Imagination 90

The Orange Story 91

Tomorrow Is the Morning 92

Musical Symphony..............................93

Meaningful Salvation 94

Stealing Love.....................................95

Art by Your Side.................................96

A Hungry Poem..................................97

Before Humanity Melts.........................98

Paperback Heart.............................99

Sky of Inner Vastness........................100

Bringing You Close..........................101

I Stand Still 102

Inner Dimension 103

No Autumn Is Devoid of Memory.............104

Dog-eared Time 105

Wilderness Has No Morality 106

Flowery Ideals 107

Vase of Passion 108

Newly Found Land 109

Fashion of Sadness 110

Self-created World 111

Depth of Subjectivity 112

Free My Cage 113

In a Poetic Manner 114

Service Is Dharma 115

Selling and Buying Time 116

Prophecy 117

Belonging to the Same Basket.................118

The Walking Rebel 120

Quietness & Slipping Time 121

Spring of Love 122

Unexplored Cave of My Library 123

Social Gaze...124

Unfathomed Hues 125

Honey..126

A Curtain with No View 127

How Fate Is Written.................................128

My Hero 129

Stooping for Love.....................................130

Footsteps of Love 131

Pushing Away 133

Art of Living

I would carry your emotions,
would you read my art?

Friendship

We will befriend each other
before destiny separates us.

Death

Set me free,
I will live before turning in my grave.
Death is my infinite time.

Bird in the Sky

If I am mesmerized by your color
will you sing while leaving?
Leave me the address where you will fly to.

The Presence of the Damned

Skin separates you and me.
This presence is a void
I continually desire our kingdom that banished me.

A Monument of Meaning

I found consciousness and
learned to play with it
my whole life.

Freedom

If I let the desire to be free extinguish,
then I agree to this universal verse.

Seclusion

I have found myself in solitude,
every soul needs to hear itself.

Readers

Carry along the unwavering quest
discovering the answers
to your legends.

Shaking Hands

If just shaking hands means friendship
why do men dine at a fancy restaurant?

All the Way

I ventured in search of my heart.
Your judgmental sermons cannot set me free.

Without You

Life has its own outlaw garage
and I keep rethinking within it.

Banishing Desires

Intellectuality is my error
if used to mend the truth.

Fame

I clean my mirror daily,
my eyes can lie.

Taking Opportunities

A simple stream flows
and invites you to wake up under the spell.

Efforts Underway

If success is a rose
I wander aimlessly in the garden
for all seasons,
drawn close to the reasons I live.

My Temptations

Sorrow is a key
to imagine a contented Sisyphus.
I drink his hemlock for not
corrupting the youths.

My Slumber

I am a resting pool
inviting swimming stalwarts.
And I am the nature, seasons have their slumber
to flower like festive delights.

My Pedestal

Refuse to say the truth does not exist—
instead, listen closely and inspect the voices.

Letting Go

When the tyrants win
they ask you to let go of your failure.
They forget life is a long walk,
before you learn to love.

The Grass Is Always Green

In my rusty alchemy, or
in the nascent rebellion
no bloodstains should be my stance.

Cloudy Haze

If you act falsely
it is an irony—
acting is only first degree mimesis;
when it is false, there is no mimesis.

Hunger

The false critics of time
desire to be fed more.

My Carrier

I have found how to live life
you only keep toying with the why,
for the hidden treasure.

Confession

I confess my guilt at the temple,
I cannot lie when I confess—
I offer my truthful guilt to the supreme one,
am I a devotee?

To Keep Moving

My boat arrives at the shore
as I reach one more chapter of my life.

My Love

The world has colors to be loved,
and pain has its own sky.

Tiredness

I am taking this turn;
I am tired of this resting habit.

Poverty

I live in an old house,
but read new books.

Poetry

Now that I can touch my sadness
and life is a journey of expression,
happiness is only an invention!
The journey is my poetry.

Love

Take me to your heart,
there is a dance that accompanies the rain.
I am a wanderer
singing my song
and losing my heart.

Agony

When I lost my home,
I started seeking the world.

Dream

I want to wake up
and embrace my reality.

Explanation

I live,
that is my explanation
to life.

Smile

My heart can hold
what my eyes desire
in the world.

Perspective

It varies by the
lives you choose to live.

The Last Rebel

If I could sell all my sadness, next I would buy happiness.

Addiction

Through the door,
a whole new version of me
is walking out.

Writing

My mind is a wildflower,
the task is to taste the honey
dripping from concrete hearts.

Sadness

Sadness is dark,
but there is moonlight for
the dark night.

Life

I made a world
out of my entire life.

Habit

Why not write every day,
and discover what happens to the ordinariness?

Discovery

Every page deserves to be turned
before the book of life ends.

Endurance

Have you tried living out on the streets?

The Age

How new is the newspaper?

Health

The crowded ways
separate for the ambulance.

Books & My Thoughts

I love to sit around books.
I will wait for the inking
of my words as long as they accompany me
to conquer my thoughts and
set them free.

Ruled by Clowns

I need reason,
I need rhyme,
only when the Piper's down
and one who rules is the clown.

Bouquet of Life or Death

Take me on a journey,
to lift me out of life.
I don't want to become a clock on the wall and age
when I can be a wallflower
and be plucked through happiness
and sorrow,
like a bouquet of life
or white consolation spread
over the grave.

When Words Make Love

These abstract words,
these exclamatory feelings,
these blue inked love letters
and first stolen glances,
they make up fine
exchanges of heart.
And when words make love
a Poet is born.

Cup of Loneliness

Let life play
and move you
to the core of the living game.
It will be easy
once you are habituated.
Silence is costly
unless it makes you
less lonely.
I come to the river
to cast away
my empty gazes.
I am a bizarre coherence,
I seek help
in enmity.
Is this the cup of loneliness?

January Winter

Wintering is an art.
When the winter sun
kisses the earth
its light *parda* seeks
an embrace.
Memories are the trust
that seek the warmth.
The mirror lake
freezes,
yet I play with
the candle
of my frosted memories.
You develop into soul
that seeks my sight,
I carry your heart
and hear all its anticipations
that embrace that forgotten book
of wintry recollections.
January winter is a memory book.
The snow falls
from the apple tree,
I cherish my fireplace
and the nostalgia.
I fondly remember you
peeling layers of winter
from my heart.
Now, you are a frozen lake -
a mirror that I carry
in my soul.

Expensive Humanity

I look at the troubles of the world
I seek a healing air.
I am a cart of agony
shoved places.
Keep a flower
at my bosom
and kiss my wounded heart.
I think humanity
is holy
for good reasons.
I carry the weight
of the aging world.
It is in my nature
to inquire about
the battlefield,
where I will not win humanity
at its own conquest.
Instead, I will be the healing mantras
for creation,
I know how
costly humanity
is becoming.

~ Sushant Thapa~

The Common Rain

If you are a seeker,
it is better not to hide.
Extend your arms
to the world,
study its people.
Feel the gravity of thoughts.
The high rising epics
all bow down to humanity.
No flower is devoid
of love.
A listening heart
is a gradual music;
an art for your
craving soul.
Refresh these notions
in a fog.
Watch the moonlight
bleeding through wine
glasses,
Wine is the blood
of the commons
Step out for
the common masses.
Like the soil,
be a lodge for earth.
I would lay my head down
and pray for rain
in parched lands.

Loving Someone

Betraying your soul
for someone's love
is against humanity's springtime.
You can still flower
even if you are stilted
in a broken pot.

Time That Followed Me

I left the analog watch behind,
but time still
followed me.
I left the digital watch behind
but time still
tickles my life.
I battle against sleeping life.
I need time to be the path finder
as I dig my furnace to know
the warmth of life.
Time conjoined me
with your serenity,
I got an outlook
to gather honey
from the hive of life's
adventure.

Crafting Love

I take a walk
this loving heart
misses your affection.
In a public park
decorated with nature,
the spring is my kiss,
the autumn is my departure
I am a lonely soul,
only you can bloom
by my iron heart.
You are the carpenter
of my craft.
Although this word "carpenter"
might sound incorrect
in a love poem.
I am a truthful bliss
with a dewdrop memory
that will make my feet wet
in the morning glory
of winter.

Holding Love Souls

Unaware, he plucks
the soul flower.
He skips reading
his horoscope
and chooses the life
that needs gardening.
An orange sky
peels its layers of colors.
Observing the sky
is like being in the immensity
of the sea.
The land is missed.
Like colorful art
abstraction isn't a distraction.
It is holding
love souls in infinite hours.
The footsteps dare
to echo in the skyway
of affection.

Looking at the World

I thank the world
but its colors are fading.
I still write freely
about the dark night,
as if I will be
filling my life with colors.
I fill my void like a well
I wish I could draw
the ink from the blue sky,
and narrate the suburban morning
to the unwatchful night
the city's lights shining,
but souls bleeding.
New lights
have old stories.
I carry the heart of snow
and wait to behold
the child of spring,
my master left
a trail,
that I follow in the darkness,
I wish to emerge
out of the blue despair
counting the stars
does not make one wise.
The world has its fortune wheels
but the vehicle is parked.

Such Winter

The water is freezing,
there is an outbreak of laziness.
I have a youthful sensation rising.
we had a battle
for love.
You see the irony.
I care for a plant
and it flowers.
I care more
and it withers like time.
A smile is a dream
for the life of tear.
I met you
and unexpected happiness
brought me the spring of kisses.
I was in a battle
for love—such ironical longings
have taken my youth away.
I have forsaken
rich man's gold
and bought myself
how much land
I need.
The graveyard isn't a home
but it is the winter of heart
I am afraid of.

A Poem in the Dark

In the dark
music plays.

In the brightness
my heart goes silent.

Shadows on the wall
remind me of you.

The landscape lightens
and I move within.

Keys type,
I have lost the feeling of ink
on my frozen fingers.

I gift a candle because
you do not invite me for candlelight dinner.

This poem is like a handkerchief
you forgot to carry,
but you always needed.

Childhood loses the chance
to become a child again.

We will meet at crossroads.

Theatre full of Love

Taking a day off
I cuddle
in our garden.
I have a flower
of your affection
that kisses me.
We spent our spring
in the garden of our love.
It is easy to
go astray and misread
love signs.
We enter the empty
theatre left all
for yourself.
You are my love queen
who can act.
I am your company of
measureless Kingdoms.
I act with you
while you act for yourself.
I am glad to accompany you
in a theatre full of audience.

The Family Photo Album

The family photo album
was already there
before I was born.
My grandfather
was already a storyteller
before he told me
vivid stories.
The photo album
became mine too,
when without me
being aware
it displayed my childhood.
I have a history too,
my own family photo album
became my past,
I rediscover the joy
of my childhood hours.
My past life comes
like a whistling train
rolling down the bend.

Beholding Love

Love escapes through
long intervals of touch
between fingers.
Kisses grow old
like mirrors
throughout life.
I was a spring dancer
now I am
a winter statue.
Clouds have darkened
and sprinkles of misty rain
fall and keep falling.
Love is an abstract noun,
but I miss your touch.
We are
concrete manifestations.
Our kisses are absolute;
they don't empty like
filled vessels.
I feel your absence
and you emerge out
of mirror frames.
I watch you
in the mirror;
we have exchanged
ourselves.

Sorrow Is a River

Morning manifests
in clean attire
as if a slate
has been washed.
The night has lost
its own caricature.
I see that the sun
has hidden itself
and winter has flowered.
The dew covered grasses
feel as if spring
has kissed them
silently.
Invention lies in
inventing happiness.
Sorrow is a river;
it drowns you
unless you learn to swim.

Art and Discontents

A fresh beginning
begins with new sights
or new insights.
Every walk of life
leads to present time.
I see myself orienting
to the artistic canvas,
pouring myself out
in scars of colorful splashes.
Resting bones
leave the flesh.
I sense a reasoning
that questions
every other question.
Buried lies
do not sprout truths
that heal.
What good is art
if it does not revive
passion and its discontents?

Favorable Conditions

I am looking
at the inner life
of a wintry afternoon.
I see my old age
in my father's eyes.
"Do you feel
motherly embrace
in your nest?"
I ask the young bird of
the early morn.
It says flying lessons
are best learned
in a stormy sky.
I don't blame
my weakness,
but learn to
aim right
and not wait for
any favorable
conditions.

Multifaceted Life

No rules can tame me.
An excuse to agreement
is a disagreement for me.
The sky falls
and the ground
touches greater heights.
How emotion dances
in the wild.
How the air whispers
a carefree routine to live.
The aquatic
takes delight
except the unseen tears.
Somewhere a night breaks
and somewhere
morning hour delights.
Some walk
some ride.
The blue is peace
the red is bold.
Life knocks,
someone leaves
the longing in life
finds rest
under the Banyan tree.
A window shouldn't be
Sightless.

The doors need to welcome
even while closing,
in order to make sure
no hard feelings
get a room.

Claps from Strangers

There are days
like lonely nights.
The company leaves
behind the nostalgia,
life is a game
to know
that you never know
how things work out.
you set up the stage
and craft an invitation letter,
the show will invite
claps from strangers—it is
a great irony.
Joy and expression
go hand in hand,
success should not
measure happiness
so you write
and bleed.

Reason to Love

Kissing the wind
I plant a seed.
You grew like apocalypse
from my parched lips.
I had no cost to live
but a reason to love.
Loneliness
does not need a voice
to show its presence.

Wind: A Musical Healer

Lost in the windy appearance
an inner beauty fades.

Taking a turn
a loveless leaf
blows.

The roots call for inclusivity.
I take a wandering stroll.
A mystic forest grows for the day,
and night leaves the sky open
to interpretation.

Among the stars
helping hands appreciate
the painting of the sky.

The leaf accompanies the wind,
wind is a musical healer.

Majestic in Absence

I want to leave
the tracks behind.
Love ages like wine.
The raisins in the sun,
the carpenter's craft
build playful carts.
Sharpening the life
the tools get blunt.
You were my reflection
of a fiery silence.
Rebellious sun
douses the winter.
You came uninvited
and lasted for a lifetime.
I could not wait for
more aging of the wine.
Love poems come
like delights of spring.
Love cannot be
a deathful sorrow
that is majestic
in absence.

Let Me Feel Alive

Let me feel alive;
I will think of the end
only at the end.

Let me love my family;
I will fall in love with a beloved
only at the end.

Let me dwell afar,
contentment is what I seek.

In humanity and its wounds
I will play the soothing tune.

Curse me with words, I will rise like air.
Curse me with words, I will answer in verses.

Swimming Waters

I took a turn
never an agony cage
that cannot be broken,
but a wandering mind.
Freedom walks
and splendid vistas appear.
Studying faces on the road
conquers the inner grief.
Strangers being social
is the feeling
of being less strange.
Some days the rain speaks
of the shelter.
Some other days
something cooks up
in the literary kitchen.
Mind has its shelter
the joy is expressive in its
swimming waters.

Nectar of Imagination

My coffee is over
and I grow old
each second.
Yet, I live
in recollections
and anticipations.
Music plays at the café
where I drop by
to find you sitting alone
waiting for some golden sun.
Last night was a celebration
of the future,
I was late
and stuck in the past.
I see you
wherever I visit.
You visit me
when I close my eyes.
I see you reading
in the sunny garden,
The bees become your
admirer,
and you a nectar of
my imagination.

The Orange Story

Someone picked up
orange from my
silver tray.
I lost my warmth
in the sun
where I would spend
my winter afternoons,
eating oranges.
I lost the afternoon.
No oranges are left
in the refrigerator
and the house
is locked
from the outside.
My orange
became the setting sun.

Tomorrow Is the Morning

Music wafts from
the open theatre.
I watch you
and sketch your picture
with all my artful recollections,
later on.
We both choose silence
to fill it
and not to be silenced.
the embrace is an art
Like the desire
to listen
the beats of a telling heart.
A poem is your eye
where I watch myself
in being you,
as I watch you.
In my embrace of the night
you are the morning
that grows from within.
Today is the night
tomorrow is the morning.

Musical Symphony

Whole day
I spoke with
your statue.
I searched my art
with a tempting heart
to find the ashes
of your traces.
The days are worn out
love is a poem
and it speaks
in volumes.
Take me away
to the distant murmurs
of the waterfall.
I could speak
with the muse,
fall in love
with your blues.
I gifted you a guitar
now you gift
me musical symphony.

Meaningful Salvation

I am going to smooth my flow
the glow isn't at the cost of time.
The lights are shining bright
when the days are flickering.
Lights know the day
although darkness needs the light.
Philosophical smoke
does not cage my faculty of mind.
I don't burn the effigies of reality,
I suspect the everyday chaos
like the puddles on the road,
any seasonal turn
can bring the mood changes,
a personal door to perception is
a freedom wind,
yet the world burns in the pyre
for meaningful salvation.

Stealing Love

When winter troubles
spring is in acceptance.
Seekers of the fog
have a wooden heart.
All the appreciation
of winter
is beside a glowing campfire.
The frost on the windowpane,
the rings of smoke
blowing from each mouth
escapes with the acceptance
of winter.
Finding a self of spring in you
would leave love marks,
this skin is a blank diary.
Let the ink of love
spread like an umbrella sky.
I found you spinning in silence
I weaved you in anticipation,
you revealed a glance,
I stole the love.

Art by Your Side

With you by my side
I could erase the nectars
and still be content.
Soaking my soul
a flower blooms
and everything is soaked
in dewdrops.
I steal the garden of your heart
and find my art
in the sun baked home.
Carry me away
to the castaway blues,
the days of belonging
to the nostalgic herds
tune my musical life.
Rhythm is the only blissful
repetition.
Love is a holding of hands
that never leaves
without memories.

A Hungry Poem

A poem for my dinner table
is hungry.
I like to summarize my day
at the family gathering
around the dinner table.
I swear my love
hangs like the blue sky,
I wake up under it
and my hunger is for a companion.
Sometimes I am right,
sometimes I am wrong,
a mystic love
would soothe my wide open eyelids.
In memory the heartache fades.
I am obliged by the hunger
to love.
I desire more love
the water pitcher
doesn't erase my thirst.
The dinner table
is a resting ground.
I dance on it,
and miss you
under the shredded sky.

Before Humanity Melts

From the ethereal
I pluck a rose
like the incantation
that reads my horoscope.
The grip and tone
of any idea
is its meaning.
Not lost in the abandonment
spontaneity is a green lawn.
The seafaring outwardness
is a treasure dove
that pecks at its alms;
someone has to
light the candle
before humanity melts.
In closed rooms
and delights of despair
an ink scripts
the fateful reality
of the running time.

Paperback Heart

Let me be damn true,
a brutal force
I come seeking the embrace.
You just trespass.
I failed to love
a lover
but that still
makes me a lover.
Damn true this heart
beats like a tale telling heart.
Love is a forgotten tale
still it keeps manifesting
in memory and everyday chaos.
The city speaks
of tattered walls
and mind capturing allegiance
of modernity.
Every world is a Wi-Fi
no one seems to write
lonely love letters now.
No one reads a paperback heart
with hardbound love,
something greater always
follows the heart,
but no audience is
part of poetry.

Sky of Inner Vastness

Sky is a divinity
it is a wish of abundance.
I walk out of my aesthetic collage
and script the longings.
Accepting the melancholy
I want to tune a true harp.
In completion
the house becomes home.
Falling in love and affection,
care and wisdom showers
perfume of colorful abundance.

Bringing You Close

I brought you close
to the bosom of rich joy.
You left in an awakening.
The thorn is no more a bouquet
even in an imaginary touch.
Pain changes the seasonal artist
and he colors the melancholy.
A new way becomes the highway
once it is accepted.

I Stand Still

I am a tree:
I have heights to attend
and yet I am a seed to be stepped by
the boot heels of burden.
Art is my way
to the salvation.
I keep the wayfarers
you have the piper,
and those that seek have dreams.

Inner Dimension

Mind is a cooking pot
hunger is for the body.

I wake up to the light
like every darkness that passes away.

Some wordplay, some thrilling insights
a wild play isn't a strict parade.

Time is a healer
gifting every day.
The ordinariness is lifted
like a winning cup filled up to the brim,
A slight perspective changes the seasons
for tremendous good,
in what you feel.

The inner dimension is a reservoir well.
Rules make a man,
passion builds immortals.

No Autumn Is Devoid of Memory

Let the breath of life
be soft like the sand on the beach.
The setting sun is an orange curtain.
Memory is a gifted painting.
Days and nights
grow like the breath of survival.
I take an idea and paint it
I wake up under the spell of the night.
My moon is the night's sun
it lets me romanticize with the night.
The spring falls like nectar
no autumn is devoid of memory.

Dog-eared Time

Music speaks
what the heart feels.
There are ways that lie
and truths that are concealed.
The morning rays
wake up with greetings of harmony.
I take up a tour in my mind
my friends cheer the emptiness
the fire in the hearth
cooks smile that brews by the heart's café.
Winter has its warmth
like a turning of the page,
life runs through the dog-eared time.

~ Sushant Thapa~

Wilderness Has No Morality

Carry me home to my kin
I have a loaded burden of the world.
I am a decorated library
yet a curious sentence,
yet to be scripted.
Metaphors speak;
questions are like reflections.
I am not a whole
yet a self under construction.
Life is in living,
I say Passion is a form of action.
Life is a liberty
the perfection bar is no measure
for happiness,
life is stepping out
from the comfort zone,
out there the wilderness has no morality.

Flowery Ideals

Take a free flowing idea
and no need to make it a river.
Engage in expression
no need to memorize the truth.
Work with passion
no need for rigid ideas,
peace is in handling the present
it is the confession of a weary-eyed traveler
he brings stories from afar.
I have heard the unheard melodies
and poet John Keats was right in its musical essence.
Take away the bells of disharmony
no temple cages the god as
faith blooms like nectar
among humanity.
Even concrete is decorated
with flowery ideals.

Vase of Passion

When I was away
I was still
attached like a free kite.
Now,
the ground is a playful parade.
Home is a world
in itself.
A complete whole is a value
of zero.
A born artist
is a child that grows
with all the tools
of an aesthete.
Appreciation is a boon
to the aesthetic ink
that announces its arrival.
Socialization does not
destroy the vase
of passion.

Newly Found Land

After Mir Taqi Mir

Drops of blood
fall from the eyelashes—this longing is a deadly disease.

The pandemonium heart is a curse of love.

Love cages the beloved
and ceases to be the order of heaven.

We are like the potter's wheel,
after our fall from the Garden of Eden.

I surmise a sky
where my shrine
is a temple of offerings—you are my queen.

I free the love
from timelessness.

Let me remain me
and let you remain you
so that we can kindle
the love, like a newly found land.

Fashion of Sadness

There is a fashion of sadness
that falls down
in every corner and main road,
I betray the sadness
and the winter sun
is not shy anymore.
I have a fire within
the sun is just a sight.
Life is a running stream
it is a devouring of the sadness.
I try to be happy all the time
and my sadness isn't an effort.
I learn the grief in the world
and labor to crush my grapes
for the wine sweeter than the grapes
in the vine.
An outlook gives me a way
someone rightly said,
"My destination isn't a place
but a new way of seeing things."
I say my happiness is a new way
of seeing things.

Self-created World

Days and dates,
faces and memories
all are reflected
like a passing train,
in moments
of thoughtfulness.
Shadows and sunlight,
time and absence
all have imprints
of thoughtfulness.
A circle is complete
in its own,
but we assign it the
value of zero.
There is a
game of perception,
making new levels
about human understanding.
Winning or losing
is like dedicating hours
of passion,
to find a space
in the self-created new world.
Self-created world
contains the entirety
in its essence.

Depth of Subjectivity

Coming from the depth
I seek.
I was on the surface
before my time disfigured.
Changes bleed.
Freedom is my luxury;
I need to proclaim freely.
A subjective flower
is my worship
of a disfigured time.
I have grown faith
overtime,
like a deep well.
Human relation
is where my empathetic spear
teaches me to hunt,
for the survival.
The first worldly lesson
has always been survival,
now we are stepping onto
new planets of discovery.

Free My Cage

I am touched
by the wind,
the gentle kiss by it,
the slow
whispering sermons
by it, on how lighthearted
I need to play the game
of life.
Every soul that blesses
me is a flower
of wild ecstasy.
The wind is my preacher.
I rise with waking alphabets
to sew my poetic patches.
Every savoring glance
frees my cage.

In a Poetic Manner

I keep looking
at the touch of a raindrop
how a lily would glow.
I kept teaching a lesson
on how to be carefree
as a child,
even in older days.
I keep cuddling
like a sweet sleep.
Music is my spontaneity
in listening to the inner city
of my being.
My inner city
is full of mind-leaves.
The echo of laughter
is my forest.
I am drunk in spontaneity
I never know how high
I can get intellectually,
in a poetic manner.

Service Is Dharma

I take a walk,
every nomenclature
seems right.
Quite a depth
speaks in observation.
Life has different names.
I am the vessel
filled with water
Kept on the sidewalk
of the road
left for animals,
on the vessel it has been carved
"Service is Dharma."

~ Sushant Thapa~

Selling and Buying Time

The office hour
isn't a foe,
but time is freedom too.
Let the office not buy your time
but try to be productive
throughout the timeline.
Time is sold and bought
freedom is caged,
if the wealth buys your time
it cages your freedom.
Work with ease,
and space.
Feel the breeze pass by.
Let the wine of passion
be your guiding force at work.
I am not against time
and office hours
but let the work enlighten
your heart.

Prophecy

The morning comes
like my arrival
to a garden.
The red carpet of assurance
tries to find
what the cause for frozen
traveling feet is.
Out there
the sun sinks swiftly
like a diving bird
reaching a nest beyond
the welkin's trauma.
I sit and watch
like a silent spectator,
why mother earth wails,
with her humanity
by her side?
A scar is something
which is deep.
Every day the morning comes
I feel like some soothing,
some consoling prophesy
will rain someday.

Belonging to the Same Basket

Rousing anthem out of silence
the music section of a mall
is pulsating like growing
meditative happiness.
What silence begets
is a cost
unless the rain is musical.
Reading Teju Cole continues
with a headphone on.
The Open City
is like a Flâneur
of Walter Benjamin.
My city also wakes up
with me
it extends like a branch of
caressing flower pot that
hangs in silence,
in the living night
that is dead without
me switching it on and off
just to commemorate
my tribute to hungry eyes
of passers-by
so their shadows speak.
I bring them inside my room
in my act of
playing with the switches
while playing with the night.

Light is a distance
to imagine
loveless mirror
kissing your parched lips.
You are my reader,
I am Teju Cole's reader,
this is a word hegemony
that rains snowflakes of freedom.
I walk beside my gazes
looking every motes
and seeing only my life awaking.
The slumber of time
needs to dress now.
I feel the music of the crowd,
there is a festive curtain billowing
one chapter of people,
next the unread chapter
in a human basket.
The separation bleeds in
timeless recollections,
is timelessness not life beyond death
that is saved from hunger?
I search love in a time frame
when I am an outlaw soul,
reaching the purgatory.
Life is made of fragments
to sit and relax,
the knife cannot cut the mind.

The Walking Rebel

The walker falls
and emerges victorious,
learning to pluck the sun
like a bouquet out of every day.
The crawlers
pursue tirelessly
to walk like the sun.
The sun does not have to fall.
The walk
is a logo of a rebel
taking the world in stride.
I enjoy walking
to my job as a lecturer
before I fall on the bog
of "Materiality"
inside my imparting English class.
As I walk the stairs for towers of progress—
the travails of mindful revolution
is casted as a reality.
Every revolution is staged
first on the streets—I
love the freedom to walk,
on the way
it feels like every day is a holiday.

Quietness & Slipping Time

I am the quietness
of the moon,

still a spot
in the earthly night.

Footsteps are anticipated
to return.

It is the midnight departure
somewhere,
heard in silence.

My dream is a memory
of long kissed sunsets
when the day bade its goodbye.

Falling and dripping,
the silence floats
in paper boats and
childhood extravaganza.

Beholding the nectar of petrichor
the midnight theatre
is an escape
from the layers of
slipping time.

Spring of Love

I have frozen fingers.
I steal the fire
from your heart
and write my love is a spring.
This free verse
has spontaneity
which is like the cascade
of rhythmic rain.
The spreading music of rainfall
has been my consoling heartbeat.
You arrive like rainbows
clad in the blanket of spring.
I flower for your art,
Come, let's embrace the shortcomings
of this longing.
Forever the world lives on
and in losing you
I lose the world.
The sky is my canvas
where your eyes are like
the sun and the moon.
Your love twinkles in the night
and I miss it like the embrace
of the day.

Unexplored Cave of My Library

Every night there is me
and every night
there is my library.
I act free, caged in my phone
the library remains untouched.
The lights are shining bright
in my library,
I lie down and enter the whirlwind of thoughts,
I want to feel the touch of every black letter.
The time rushes like a bullet train
as untouched deadlines arise out of the casket.
Life is a slow progression.
I wish to cast my will
to my library and travel in its unexplored cave.
Slowly I rise.

Social Gaze

Come take me
to the majestic soaring heights.

I have fathomed an ounce of meaning
out of this routine.

Bore me not till death arrives,
I invite the mystic trance.

Healing life is like a moonrise,
the aura beside the bed
with bleeding moonlight
takes me to eternity.

Like kissing jasmine
the spring leaves its mark,
love blooms when the soul is touched.

Come take me
to the refrain of life,
where happiness repeats and speaks
of the future.

This road is my companion
the passers-by hold the key
to my social gaze.

Unfathomed Hues

Life is a musical departure.
Either there is music in recollection
or notes of longings, in departure.
Our soft kisses
invite winter embraces.
This erasure of time
treasures love's garden
where the purple hibiscus
is not blood red—even the sunshine
does not stay the same.
Hearts darken their colors
while in love,
the purple hibiscus is my excuse
to love you,
with unfathomed hues,
of musical sunsets.

Honey

Again the morning shines.
I can listen
more to music.
The sun takes a supreme flight.
I watch with holy eyes
I kiss your belief,
a butterfly flies
from your lips
holy like the worshipping sun.
The yellowness
feels close.
Winter is affection,
it is the season
to come closer.
No more prosaic eyes
can seek
the beauty in the world.
Poetry rains
like honey,
music tames
the bleeding heart.

A Curtain with No View

Life is a beautiful reality
but there are crossroads.
Journey can outlast
as it can also recollect.
Decisions are important,
I learn from a commoner,
and they roam in my verses.
There is no mask of absence,
love is a shy flower
kissing the winds.
The world itself is a love delight;
sometimes sad tides
touch the sea.
War and its aftereffects
make personal life
a shade of a curtain
with no view.

How Fate Is Written

The darkened scraps
of horoscope
burn your childhood,
if your childhood
was nothing
but dependent
on astrology.
The approaching adulthood
for you would be nothing but
dependent docile shadow
of astrology.
"Everything is written in fate,"
"Become a fate writer and
let the fate write
poetry for you," so-called
ancestral voices
would prophesize.
I heard my fate was
half written, and I myself
have to write how it ends,
and so, I champion it
with this life—
fate is an unseen mirror.

My Hero

When I see you unguided
without paths measured with reason
you still move the whole sea
without touching its shore.
You create the banks of the rivers when
you want to step out of the water.
You act without consent
and that has also made you free;
for you worship time and work.
Cutting every rope that pulled you back
you swallow the earthen planet.
You are a reason's delight
a heart in a waking life.
You are of the land and
you make the sky immortal
because your gaze exists far and near.
The spirit of voices in you
have driven the chariot of minds in others.
You are my verse of faith;
my hero of words and deeds.
You are my simple idol
not made of voiceless stones.
You are also the reader of this verse
among the poets of the world.
You are living and yet divine;
yet abstract and running like blood;
above all you are human.

Stooping for Love

I forgot how
love is pronounced
and now a lake
has found its way
to drown me.
I look up to the world
and steal a shawl.
I lift
a shy cup
of forgiveness
and remember that
one cannot
seek forgiveness
until it is willed.
Have I reached
somewhere high above
to the world of love
or has the world
stooped for love?

Footsteps of Love

I invite you
to miles and miles
of promised lands.
I kiss the togetherness
of dawn and dusk,
stitched by longing
to be one in this shredded world.
I pause in my life
to give a glance at the love
you bring,
like the jubilant rain
bringing the dance home.
I am a free soul,
a divine being who spilled
in solitude the meaning of life.
It still trickles like honey
and some musical geometry.
The winter is fading away
there is no agony that burns
in the fireplace,
I lift an empty cup
and ask life,
can we give birth
to a third heart of love?
You and I,
and fill it to the brim
to ease the thirst
of togetherness.
Solitude is silent enough
to hear the music

that brings
footsteps of love.

Pushing Away

I feast inappropriately
and postpone working days
enslaved by constant
Digital Surveillance
day by day.
More working lies grow
like lilacs out of the dead.
This life has been a text
and its ashes
are being grown.
Something literary
arises like massive waves
and the sunken ship
somehow finds its way.
I find each morning musical
the night feels
as if no sleep
needs to be unembraced.
Is it a happiness rising
or a cursed age
where screens
are worshipped?
Lovers approach
with open arms,
the habitual solitude pushes
them away.
Literariness is a curse
sometimes,
again I remember
life is an abstract noun
and it will go on.

www.ingramcontent.com/pod-product-compliance
Lightning Source LLC
Chambersburg PA
CBHW060443040426
42331CB00044B/2595